HOW TO BREAK INTO THE FILM BUSINESS

The Production Assistant Handbook

by

Jeff Alves

Edited and Foreword by
William-Alan Landes

PLAYERS PRESS

HOW TO BREAK INTO THE FILM BUSINESS

First Edition 1991

ISBN 0-88734-616-2
Library of Congress Catalog Number: 91-52900

PLAYERS PRESS, Inc.
P.O. Box 1132
Studio City, CA 91614-0132

Printed in the U.S.A.

Library of Congress Cataloging-in-Publication Data

Alves, Jeff.
    How to break into the film business : the production assistant
handbook / by Jeff Alves ; edited and foreword by William-Alan
Landes.
        p.   cm.
    ISBN 0-88734-616-2 (pbk.)
    1. Motion pictures--Production and direction--Handbooks, manuals,
etc. 2. Motion pictures--Production and direction--Vocational
guidance.   I. Landes, William-Alan.   II. Title.
PN1995.9.P7A47   1991
791.43'0232'023--dc20   91-52900
                                                                CIP

FOREWORD

There are numerous books about the glamour of the entertainment industry; stars abound, the rich and famous are everywhere. We all seem to enter the industry blinded by stardust, armed with misconceptions and driven by youthful overconfidence. It's a beautiful dream. I did it just this way. I finished school and headed to the West Coast from New York; I was confident that anything I hadn't learned would be of minimal importance and that on the set and in the screening room I'd pick it all up.

It was never that easy. Over the years, again and again, I've heard *"my story"* from the famous and the forgotten whether actor, director, technician, or crew member. We each seem to learn, sometimes too late, that there is more to know than we have learned. The difficult part is where to find this information.

There are very few good books that meticulously outline the specifics, accurately and realistically on what really is necessary, to fulfill and acquire specific jobs within the industry. There are even fewer books that bridge the gap of formal education and professional training. Whether you consider the Production Assistant position as a starting or entry job, a stepping stone up the production ladder to director or producer, or an important career within the production community, this book has the information you need.

Jeff Alves, Production Assistant/Coordinator who carefully documented his learning experiences, has truly brought a greater clarity to one of the significant areas of the entertainment industry. His book not only details the starting *how-to* for Production Assistants but it is a continual working handbook that everyone working on or in a production should read and re-read. The information outstrips just the Production Assistant; it is an invaluable reference for Production Manager, Stage Manager,

Producer, Director, and even Actor. It guides you through the miriad of mazes within the industry and clearly outlines, in detail, the working production from start to finish.

I remember working for Marvin Miller and we had a star actor who was late several times. Mr. Miller told me, "Look, kid. It doesn't matter how talented you are, in this business you need to show up on time and do your job." That remains one of the most useful pieces of information I ever learned on a set. It was emphasized when Mr. Miller closed the production because the star was late too often. The film was later completed but with a different star.

In the days when I first worked production, I would have given anything to have had the information Jeff has carefully presented in this book. Working with this material took me back to when I hired and worked with neophytes, of which I wasn't much more. Boy, how many questions and problems, my own included, could have been avoided had they or I read this text. Many of the people I encountered and have known might have survived the industry pitfalls and even achieved their goals or dreams, if only they had read this guide.

William-Alan Landes

CONTENTS

PART ONE

PART TWO

PART THREE

PART FOUR

PART FIVE

PART SIX

This book is dedicated to my wife, Bridget. Thanks for standing by me.

Jeff

Introduction

The entertainment industry is one of the largest— and fastest growing —— occupational fields in the world. TV and movie production companies are constantly seeking dedicated, motivated Production Assistants to enter this field. Once you have joined the fellowship of entertainment professionals, you can advance as far as your skills and knowledge will take you. This book reveals everything you need to know about becoming and being an excellent Production Assistant.

When I first started no one warned me that I needed to know both how to get a job, and, how to do it well once I got it. Since then, I haved learned many strategies for doing this highly detailed work. Before this book was published, the only way to learn these strategies was through on-the-job training that involved **much** frustration and anguish due to **wasted** effort and many mistakes.

Exactly what is a Production Assistant, and what does a production assistant do? This book will fully describe the important role of a Production Assistant in film or television. It takes you step by step through the various duties , from start to finish.

Getting started in the industry can be very difficult. The old adage about "who you know" is very apropos. If you know the right people you can quickly get a job. Can you keep it ? Will you get hired again? The answer to these questions will depend on your performance and abilities. You can know the Producer; get hired ; do a poor job and out you go. Who you know *is* important, but what you know may be more important.

If you're starting out, and don't have a "who" connection to get you that first job, how do you land it ? What you know will help, not only to make the right contacts, but also to make the contacts work to your advantage. One thing that I thought should weigh heavily would be a good film education. Now, I'm totally in favor of education ; unfortunately the classes are great for theory and techniques but no help learning the *ins* and *outs* of being on a professional production set or out on location.

The information you can learn from this book was learned by me the hard way ; long hours, good and bad experiences and by observing mistakes, my own and those of others. Despite these trials and tribulations, I passionately enjoy my work and highly recommend it to you. It has exposed me to many kinds of people and many areas of expertise in television, commercials, video and film production. I hope that this book encourages you to reap the same satisfaction in your entertainment career.

The tips and techniques I learned are offered here to help you move through the production maze. Hopefully the information presented will give you the edge needed to start working as a Production Assistant. Hard work combined with the knowledge of what is expected of you can open the door to many opportunities in this exciting industry. You can look at being a PA as a career in itself or as an entry level job that will start you on your way to a more specific crew position or to the stellar heights of Producer or Director.

© Universal Pictures - Paul Newman directing NEVER GIVE AN INCH. *Courtesy of Universal Studios.*

PART ONE

STARTING OUT

CHAPTER

1

Finding a Job:
Who and What to Look for
and Where to Look

The most important factor in getting a Production Assistant (PA) job is looking in the right place. Of the several ways to become a PA, the easiest is to know someone who is hiring a PA, the next best someone is a working PA. As I've stated, having a contact in the business is the quickest and surest way to get your start. Where you go from there is up to you.

Another way is to send your resume to a production house. This is a competitive business, and production houses welcome a resume from a hard-working, motivated self-starter. If you have prior experience, a resume can be a helpful way of communicating that to your interviewer. If you send a resume, be sure to include a well-written, enthusiastic cover letter.

A resume, however, is not essential to landing a job as a PA. One approach that works well is to walk directly into the office of a production company and ask to speak with the person in charge of hiring Production Assistants. In large companies, the Production Coordinator or Producer Manager probably hires the PAs. If the company is small, the Producer or Associate Producer may do the hiring. In some companies, the in-house Coordinator may freelance or work out of another location. Therefore, when you ask to speak with the Coordinator about seeking employment, you may be told that the coordinator is not in the office. The main object is to be in the right place at the right time.

Another way to meet the right people is to go to some working stages and to inquire about jobs there. This is a very delicate business, so use common sense when approaching a Coordinator or anyone who is busy working. Remember that first impressions are important. Most companies hire freelance crews for upcoming jobs. Freelance employees do not have permanent staff positions. Many periodicals and trade papers include sections listing companies in need of PAs and other jobs in the industry —— often an excellent source of information about prospective freelance PA jobs. It only takes a phone call to inquire about an available position.

Don't hesitate to take any work that is offered to you. What you need is experience, and one way to get it, may be by working for free. Sometimes, freebies (or "spec", as it is called) offer free "on the job training", which can help you gain experience. Though this training period is not easy, if you are committed to finding a job and are just starting out, it is an option that could be worth your time.

Inquiring about jobs also offers additional payoffs. Even if a company doesn't need anyone at this time, they may put you on a future call list or refer you to someone else who has work available. Your ultimate goal is to obtain as many names and contacts as possible. Let everybody know that you want to become a PA. You never know who you're going to meet or when you're going to meet someone who can help you.

One final way of finding a job is to look in your area's film and video production directory. * Directory's are an excellent source of information concering production companies. Call the companies you think you might like to work for. Most companies will curtly suggest that you send a resume and then quickly hang up. Send it. After sending your resume, always follow up with a phone call.

Keep a written log of who you spoke to, interviews, where and when you sent each resume, etc. Follow up with Thank You cards if someone is helpful, notes and cards that you are working; even holiday cards to help them remember you.

When you get that interview, make sure the person interviewing you knows as much about you and your background as possible. Highlight special skills and knowledge you have——— You were a waiter, teacher, cab driver —— each of these and other skills have a special importance to a production. If you have lived in the area, where the company is shooting, your familiarity with the neighborhood could be

*The *L.A. 411* is the film directory in the Los Angeles area.

an asset; you'll know the streets and save time on errands. If you have a pick-up truck or large vehicle mention it —— It's an important item that could help get you that job.

Give 110% of your effort, and show prospective employers that you are looking for a company that likes that attitude. This is a high-energy business. When speaking with people, show your enthusiasm!

CHAPTER

2

Three Kinds of Assignments:
Booked / On Hold / Half Day

"Booked"

The goal of your first job-seeking efforts is to be "booked", which means that the Coordinator has hired you for a certain number of days (that is, the number of days you and the Coordinator discussed). If you are booked, you can count on actually getting the job 99% of the time. The production assignment has been awarded to the Director, and the wheels are in motion to begin the production. The other 1% allows for the slim chance that the company's production job might not work out. If the job offer falls through, it is usually due to some sort of problem between the advertising company and the clients' product or with the production company that has hired you. This seldom happens once you have been booked.

"On Hold"

Sometimes however, the company is less certain of getting a job. Nonetheless, when you are put "on hold", the company is likely to get the job. Being "on hold" means that if the company is awarded the job, the Coordinator will use you. No guarantees come with this. Being put "on hold" is both good and bad. The good aspects are that the company wants to hire you and that you might have work lined up if the company secures the job. However, there is still the possibility the job might fall through.

There are many problems with being on Hold. You could accept the "On Hold" status and then another job comes through. You might find out about a job, after you accepted "On Hold". Do you apply ? Can you book it ? You might be offered a job that overlaps or conflicts with the "On Hold" job.

I don't believe there is any one simple answer to the above problems. Each problem can have many solutions, unfortunatety the bottom line is that you may have to pass a good job, only to find out that the "On Hold" job doesn't materialize. I recommend going after all possible jobs ; then if you book a conflict, tell both parties about the situation. Usually industry professionals will understand that a booking is better than a maybe. The real dilemma is if the "On Hold" is a big job and the booking a small one ; that's a decision you'll have to make on your own – wait and take a chance or go with the booking.

"Half-Day"

Receiving a call for a "half day" is exactly what it means. The prod-

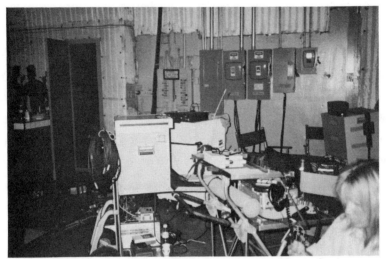

Video playback and sound equipment. Boom person prepares for the next shot on a JACK IN THE BOX spot.

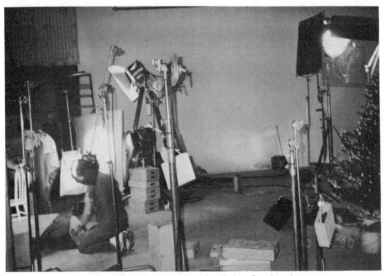

The Best Boy is tweaking the lights for the shot.

uction Coordinator only needs you for half a day (or the budget doesn't allow for a full day's expense). Though it's not ideal, it is a good way to break into a new company —— anything to get your foot in the door. There are many similarites in taking a half-day booking as in being "On Hold". You might get a call to book a full day, week etc.; there might be a chance for a better job that comes in after you booked the half-day; etc. If your'e a newcomer, chances are you won't have this problem, but after you start to work this is a serious risk. My advise is, when you start working regularly, semi-regularly, you should reconsider your career objectives and say "No" to half-days. Most Coordinators will understand.

Brenda Vaccaro (*Left*) and Jack Lemmon (*Right*) confer with director Jerry Jameson (*Center*) between scenes of "AIRPORT '77." *Courtesy of Universal Studios.*

CHAPTER

3

Union Versus Nonunion Work

Early in your career in the entertainment business, you'll find yourself discussing union versus non-union work: Why is there a union? What can it do for me? Is non-union work good? There are different unions in the commercial film business, but is there a Production Assistant's union? Yes: One such union is the National Association of Broadcast Employees and Technicians (NABET) located throughout the U.S. In the union your title is described as "utility" and not Production Assistant; though the two job descriptions are identical.

Union membership is a Catch-22 situation. You cannot work for any union house until you are in the union- *but* you cannot join the union and get all the benefits until you (1) work a certain number of hours,

(2) make a certain amount of money, and (3) do so within a specified period of time. The ideal situation for resolving this is to be hired by a union company so that you can meet the union rules for the benefits. Before paying the dues/fees to join the union, make sure a union house is going to hire you on a regular basis. The union pays an hourly wage, not a flat fee (see Part 5, "Money Issues").

The other option, non-union work, offers a lot more opportunity for work but no benefits. Individuals are usually paid on a flat day-rate, and the rate is usually lower than the union rate— but not always. Remember that when you are starting out, some work is better than no work. My recommendation is, take the work when it is offered to you. You need credits and working non-union can help build your history as well as connections.

An interesting situation exists in the Union/Non-Union controversy. Even as a union member you can still work non-union jobs. The union, obviously, does not appreciate this dual standard, but thus far they have not taken an active stand on preventing members from working non-union. Maybe, they too realize that we need to work—we would rather work union but sometimes there is no other choice but to take a non-union job.

Take a lesson from the union actress who worked non-union and then took ads to announce her work. The acting union, couldn't ignore her obvious violation of their code. If you find yourself, a union member, taking non-union work, keep it to yourself.

16

CHAPTER

4

Got The Job

Attitude

Once you are hired, you must perform-not just well, but also enthusiastically. A major part of performance is attitude. A positive attitude is one of the most important things to have as a PA. This can make or break you. It is important to have a willingness to learn and lots of energy. A winning attitude is knowing that whatever is asked of you, you will do well.

Teamwork is also essential. Be flexible with your fellow workers. It is always a team effort; production is the backbone of the industry. The accolades and praise may not be apparent, but it is heart felt. Ask yourself, "How or what can I do to make the project run smoothly ?" Then do it with a smile. A smile is a must. Tell yourself, "I've been hired for a specific job and they are paying me, so I will do the best I can and always wear a *smile*".

Special Abilities

The Coordinator hired you because of something outstanding you said in the interview or your past performance. Be aware of the special abilities that persuaded that person to hire you. Knowing what that quality is will carry you through this job and on to the next one. Try to work closely with the Coordinator, assuring the Coordinator that you have everything under control— and make sure that you do!

Protocol

Protocol is something you have to be aware of in business, and the film production business is no different. You are a neophyte, just starting in a business that has a history and goal of success. One common mistake is putting too much emphasis on what you think you know. Now is the time to understand that you may not have all the answers. Be helpful, make suggestions and always do your best. Be careful about trying too hard to be recognized—— especially trying to show off that you know a better way to do everything. When you take this"Know it all attitude", the negative can be, what you think you know isn't very much, and now everyone knows that you don't know anything. The system is really very simple. The Director is there to direct. The Grips and Gaffers are there to work with lighting and electrical. The Coordinator is there to coordinate pick-ups and deliveries of what is needed on the set. As a Production Assistant, you are expected to assist. As valuable as you may think your advice may be to others, it is probably better to keep it to yourself. Once you move up the ladder, you can do things your way, but for the time being, listen and learn, learn, learn.

There may be a time when you are asked for your opinion or ideas; this may be the time to make suggestions. Be sure your suggestions are valid.

Hertz commercial: Jeff Alves (*Center*) working as a set P.A. with O.J. Simpson, Golf great Arnold Palmer and movie and T.V. star Jamie Lee Curtis.

Hertz commercial shot in Palm Springs: Steven Buck, Assistant Director, (*Left*) walks back to Paul Guliner, Director, as Hertz clients check the last take to see if it was a print.

CHAPTER

5

Lead Production Assistant

One person from whom you can learn a great deal is the production company's lead PA. As with most jobs, there is someone who has been there before you and he or she knows a little bit more than you do. Don't feel intimidated by this. Instead, use this resource to your advantage by watching and learning. Usually, a Coordinator has a P.A. with whom he or she has worked for some time. The PA is hired repeatedly because the PA has done a great job for the coordinator. This experienced person is called the "Lead PA" or the "Head PA." Typically, the lead PA is working towards becoming a Coordinator. The lead is called to work first, at the start of the production, and serves as the right hand person to the Coordinator. The prep may include checking times and availabilities of crew members and suppliers, obtaining permits and organizing pre-pro (pre-production) meeting with clients and staff.

When the production start date gets closer, the other PAs are called in. The lead PA organizes the other PAs and makes sure that the proper things happen in the correct order. The lead has a lot of responsibility. Often, a Coordinator hires a new or green PA. It is the lead's duty to help train the new person and to guide the new person in the right ways of production. Enthusiastically learn from the guidance.

PART TWO

SHOOTING

CHAPTER

6

The Production Cycle

Knowing how a film production runs its cycle is very important. To help understand the process, I'll describe a one-day shoot (that is, one day of filming) commercial cycle. The procedure for films is very similar, but the entire cycle can span up to a year or more. The time frame for commercials is much more condensed.

Prep Day

On the *prep* day, the Coordinator and the Producer prepare for the commercial's *shoot* day. Preparation entails the Coordinator communicating with the Clients, the Agency, and the Director, discussing every detail of the commercial (making phone calls, and meeting face to face with all parties). This day requires a lot of running around, and it can be very frustrating. Nonetheless, keep smiling: You're still learning. The key is to learn as much as possible, as quickly as possible.

Shoot Day

The *shoot* day is why you are all there. It's usually an early day. Energy runs high on this day. As a PA, you will get to the stage or location before any other crew members. Here is a little tip: If you are on time, you are 15 minutes late. The performance of a PA on this day is a "trial" by the people in charge, and you should be aware of this.

Wrap Day

The *wrap* day is the day on which everything that was used is to be returned in good condition and on time. Also, this is a day on which all the loose ends get tied up. The chapters that follow will go into more detail about the prep, wrap, and shoot days. Though each aspect of the production cycle is essential, the central feature of your job is to ensure that everything goes well during the shoot. The preparation and wrap-up tasks are described fully in "Part 4 : Other Duties."

CHAPTER

7

The Shot:
The Most Important Thing

Being a PA entails multitudinous detail, from the start to the finish of production, in the office, at the shoot, and in the wrap. Nonetheless, anyone in the business will say that getting the "shot" is most important of all, even though you and many others spend long hours prepping for and wrapping after the shoot. The Camera Operator and the Director (in some cases, this is the same person) have been compiling all their ideas and are waiting to catch that magical moment on film.

Once shooting is ready to begin, the Assistant Director "AD" becomes your boss on the set. The Coordinator is the person who hired you and is your main boss, but you are there now to help everybody.

27

Sometimes you might feel that you have 4 or 5 bosses, that is not unusual. The AD is hired to get the shot completed on time, so if he or she needs help, it is your job to help. The AD, and the Coordinator know the best priorities for your time and effort. Go with the flow, and make sure you're wearing a smile. You are paid to be helpful.

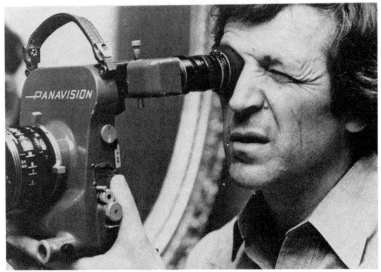

Director Costa-Gavras checks a shot for "MISSING." *Courtesy of Universal Pictures/Polygram Pictures Presentation.*

CHAPTER

8

Handling The Film

Delivering the Dailies

Dailies refer to the film that has been shot and is being developed at the lab, to be screened the next day. For example, at the end of the shoot day, the Assistant Cameraman down loads (removes for processing) the magazines (containers) of film. The Coordinator gives a *purchase order* (PO) to the Assistant Cameraman or the Second Assistant Cameraman to be filled out and attached to the cans going to the lab for processing.

The PA will receive the cans of film from the camera department to be dropped off at the lab (customer service is where the film is usually received). The lab takes 6 to 12 hours to develop the film. The next day, you will return to the lab to pick up the finished product and get it ready for screening in a screening room or on a moviola.

Racking up the Moviola

Learning to rack up the dailies onto the moviola can and *will* increase your pay rate. The philosophy here is that the more you know, the more you will be worth. Many times, you will be asked whether you know how to rack up a moviola. This takes practice to learn how to do well.

Pressures come with this job. The dailies are what everybody, including the Director, the Producer, the Coordinator, the Clients, and the Agency are waiting for. Don't sweat it. Take your time, do it right, and make sure that all the speeds are set on "slow" to start. Make sure the loops are large enough not to tear the film.

If you don't know how to rack up the moviola—— learn. Find someone who will show you, preferably on your own time. Then when the question comes up, you can say —— yes

Avoiding Hassles

Unless you specify otherwise, the film might come from the lab upside-down, "tails out" (i.e., backwards) and sometimes in ways you didn't think film could be placed on a spool. To avoid these problems, ask the Assistant Cameraman to write on the purchase order going to the lab, "Heads Out."

This means that the lab will, 99% of the time, rewind the film so it is right side up on the reel. If they do so you can quickly and easily rack it onto the moviola without having to rewind it yourself. Rewinding is a hassle and a waste of time, let the lab do it. The proper term for correctly rewound film is "the emulsion-side up, and heads out". When racking up the moviola, the black line on the film goes closest to the moviola.

Following are specific instructions and diagrams to show you *exactly* how to rack up a moviola, the information was provided by Hal Dennis Productions, Hollywood, CA.

PREPARATION FOR USE
35 MM

IMPORTANT:

1. Check for adequate loop sizes between lower feed sprocket and gate, and between intermittent sprocket and upper feed sprocket. Film loop size must be large enough to prevent film tension but small enough to prevent film rubbing against machine.

2. Turn flywheel by hand to check movement of film and film loops.

3. Remove slack between jerk absorber rollers and reels.

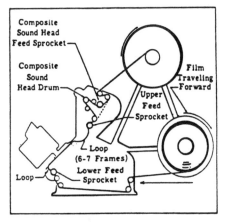

Figure 1. Film Threading, 35mm Machine

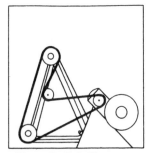

Figure 2. Belt Placement

32

Single Sound Head Machine

The center volume control knob on the main body is the sound volume control. An amplifier OFF switch is integral with the VOLUME CONTROL.

Double Sound Head Machines

On machines incorporating two sound heads, the center VOLUME CONTROL knob controls the volume as for a single sound head; in addition, each EXCITER LAMP reheostat controls exciter lamp intensity of the nearest head giving independent control of each sound head.

IMPORTANT: If only one optical sound head is in use, or if the magnetic sound is in use, be certain that the EXCITER LAMP rheostats for non-operating optical sound units are in the off position.

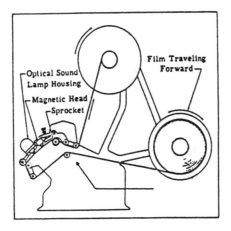

Figure 3. Separate Sound Head Film Threading Diagram

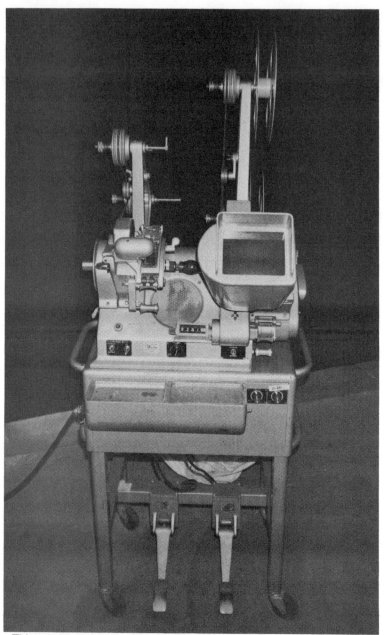

This specific machine, made by **Moviola**, is run by a motor and is generally equipped to handle a single reel of motion picture film and a single sound track.

PART THREE

TOOLS OF THE TRADE

CHAPTER

9

Equipment Bag

To do the best job possible it is imperative you have the right tools. You can usually keep your equipment in a lightweight carrying case or bag. Your equipment bag should have the following features:

1. Shoulder straps, or at least handles.
2. Easy access for opening, closing, storing, and removing equipment.
3. Lightweight but sturdy design; able to take a beating (canvas and nylon provide this characteristic, a briefcase is impractical for this reason).
4. Many compartments in which to hold serveral items separately.

As you read the list of suggested equipment, you will see why I suggest the above features for your equipment bag.

The reason to have equipment is to make your job easier and more efficient. Don't rush out and spend a lot of money that you don't have for the first job. You should, however, gradually pick up more equipment. When I first started, all I had was a piece of paper in my back pocket and a pen in my front pocket, to note names, times, and places to pick up gear. A complete equipment bag will develop over a period of time. The more equipment you have to do your job effectively, the easier it will be.

Here are a few things you should have in your bag:

1.*	*Local Street* guide		9.**	Production Directory
2.	Writing implements		10.	Note pad
3.	Padlock with a key		11.	Bottle opener
4.	Matte knife		12.	Mini stapler
5.	Self stick notes		13.	Buck knife
6.	Belt		14.	Invoice book
7.	Pocket calculator		15.	Mini mag light
8.	Felt tip markers		16.	Source book

* In Los Angeles the Thomas Brothers Guide
**In Los Angeles one directory is the LA 411.

CHAPTER

10

Paperwork

Call Sheet

It is a necessity for all PAs to know both what a *call sheet* is and how to read one. A call sheet consists of (1) the crew and their job titles (2) equipment suppliers and their phone number (3) job name and number (4) day and time (5) location of the shoot (6) Talent, etc. (See the sample "Call Sheet" at the end of this chapter).

Production Report

A *production report* is a report of the day-by-day production activities. It includes: (1) when the crew starts (2) when the talent arrives (3) the equipment used (4) type of film used, etc. It is as important as a call sheet and is usually filled out throughout the day. If there is a First AD or a Second AD, this is his or her duty; if not, the Coordinator fills it out. Try to learn how to fill this out; anything that you can learn to help a Coordinator makes you more valuable as a PA (See the sample "Daily Production Report" form at the end of this chapter).

CALLSHEET

DATE:_____

CALLTIME:____ JOB NO: _____

LOCATION_____ STAGE:_____ AT: _____

_____ PHONE:_____ PRODUCT: _____

CLIENTS _____ HOTEL:_____ AGENCY:_____

_____ PHONE:_____ DAY: _____ OF: _____

MOS   SYNC   TAPE   16MM   35MM
☐   ☐   ☐   ☐   ☐

Category	Name Phone #	Time IN	Time Out	Category	Name Phone #	Time IN	Time Out
DIRECTOR				GAFFER			
PRODUCER				BEST BOY			
DIR.PHOTO.				ELEC.			
PROD. MGR.				ELEC.			
CAMERA				KEY			
ASST.CAM.				GRIP			
ASST. DIR.				GRIP			
STYLIST				PROPS.			
MAKE-UP				PROPS.			
MIXER				PA			
BOOM				PA			
VTR				PA			

TALENT: NAME AND #	AGENCY & PHONE NO.	CALL TIME	SPOTS
1._____			
2._____			
3._____			
4._____			
5._____			
6._____			

CallSheet

JOB#   AGENCY:
                              AGENCY PRODUCER:

LOCATION:

SHOOT DAY:
                              NAME   PHONE#

EXEC. PRODUCER:
PRODUCER:
DIRECTOR:
DIRECTOR OF PHOTOGRAPHY:
ASST. CAMERA:
ASST. DIRECTOR:
GAFFER:
BEST BOY:
ELEC.
KEY GRIP:
GRIP:
GRIP TRUCK DRIVER:
STUDIO TEACHER:
PROP. MASTER:
SET. DRESSER:
SCRIPT:
SOUND:
MAKE-UP:
VTR:
WARDROBE:
PRODUCTION ASST.
PRODUCTION ASST.
PRODUCTION ASST.
CRAFT SERVICE:

DAILY PRODUCTION REPORT

ADVERTISING AGENCY:		PRODUCT AND TITLE:		DATE:	M T W T F S S

PRODUCTION #	LAB. FILM	STOCK	LAB.SOUND	LOCATIONS
TRUCK CALL		FOOTAGE EXPOSED TO DATE:		
CREW CALL		FOOTAGE EXPOSED		
1ST SHOT				
LUNCH START				
LUNCH END				
1ST PM SHOT		WEATHER:		
SUPPER START				
SUPPER END				
WRAP CAMERA				
CREW WRAP				

EQIUPMENT

CAMERA:

GENERATOR:

SOUND:

ELECTRICAL:

GRIP:

DOLLY:

WALKIE-TALKIE

TRANSPORTATION:

CATERING:

REMARKS:

DAILY PRODUCTION REPORT
(REAR)

PRODUCT:

DAY-DATE:

JOB NO.

PRODUCER:

CATEGORY	NAME	IN	L	D	OUT	CATEGORY	NAME	IN	L	D	OUT
DIRECTOR						GAFFER					
ASST. DIR						BEST BOY					
COORD.						ELEC.					
CAMERA						KEY GRIP					
SCRIPT						GRIP					
MAKE-UP						SFX					
HAIR						PROPS.					
MIXER						PA					
VTR						PA					
STYLIST						PA					

TALENT

NAME	TELEPHONE	CATEGORY	IN	LUNCH	DINNER	OUT

CHAPTER

11

Walkie-Talkies

Walkie-talkies are used to communicate with persons who can't be by your side all the time. They are used to ensure everybody involved in the production is on the same wave length. Everyone must be completely aware of what is taking place and what changes might have to be made in order for the production to run smoothly. The best example of the need for effective communication is location shooting, when the crew might be separated by one or more physical miles. If so, the walkie-talkie may be your only form of communication with others involved in the shoot.

Walkie-talkies run on removable batteries, located either on the bottom or the side of the unit. They differ in size, range, type, and style, and some are adaptable to headsets. Mountains or downtown buildings might limit the units' range or lower or even cut off the units' ability to respond. Physical obstructions might also hinder communication.

Walkie-talkies offer a valuable means of communication. Be aware that when engaging in conversation you must be direct and to the point with questions and answers; speak clearly and don't mumble. Remember, what you say can be heard by everyone.

Before handing out the walkie-talkie be sure all antennas are attached, they are turned on and that they are all set on the same channel, usually channel 1.

Keep a record of who gets each unit. Sometimes they disappear and it can be useful knowing who had it last. A good idea is to number each unit by adding a sticker; then log each unit in and out.

Below is a variety of terms that you will hear consistently, with limited variations on most sets.

WALKIE-TALKIE LINGO

Copy? or Did you copy?	- Do you hear me, clearly?
10/4	- A positive response
Copy that	- Did you hear me?
Roger that	- Understand
What's your 20	- Where are you?
Go to 2	- Switch to channel 2 on the walkie-talkie
Back to 1	- Switch back to channel 1
Hold traffic	- Don't let cars or people through

The Motorola 440 equipped with charger, holster and headset.

The Motorola PX300-S is used as a base unit, mainly on location jobs.

Release Traffic	- Let the cars and people through.
Watch your back	- Get out of the way.
Flash	- Used before an instamatic camera that has a flash attachment . (Never fire a flash when film or tape is rolling).

The Walkie Talkies pictured were supplied to us by friends at Access Communication, Hollywood, CA.

The 440 model is widely used by the film and television industry.

PART FOUR

DUTIES OF A
PRODUCTION ASSISTANT

CHAPTER

12

Obtaining Equipment and Supplies

Your role during the shoot is important, but perhaps even more important to the team effort is your role in preparing for the shoot. It is your job to see to it that all the equipment and supply needs of *everybody* on the production team are met. It can be quite a daunting task to attend to every last detail of a production site. If you can do this well, you've proven yourself indispensable to the team.

Most of the rental equipment has to be picked up prior to the beginning of the shoot and dropped off at the end. Some supplies and specialized items, however, must be picked up daily. Do this aspect of your job willingly, pleasantly, and efficiently, your efforts will be appreciated.

Though you do have to pick up and deliver all the equipment and supplies, you aren't required to order them. The Coordinator calls the *vendors* (suppliers of equipment or materials) to request the equipment. When the Coordinator orders the materials, he or she tells the supplier the specific (purchase order) number so that no two orders have the same PO number, and each purchase can be tracked individually according to the PO number.

The following are the key tasks of a PA in regard to equipment and supplies:

1. Get the POs for all the gear to be picked up in one trip (usually from the Coordinator or from accounting personnel).

2. Check out the van or truck in which the equipment is to be picked up. Make sure that you have rope and furniture pads and any other materials you might need for securely storing the gear. Don't forget gas, oil and water to keep the vehicle running.

3. Plan a route for picking up the gear (knowing the locations of vendors and the stages in the area will make your job easier) remember the *Local Street Guide* from Chapter 9.

4. Go to each vendor, present the PO to the vendor, and wait for the vendor to gather the requested items.

5. Before leaving with the item(s), confirm that each item on the PO was received and that the condition of each item was satisfactory (you're responsible for this and for returning each item in the same condition in which it was received). Assuming that all is satisfactory,

A production lighting package stored on stage.

The Grips area: C-stands, apple boxes, wedges, sandbags, etc.

you will sign a form confirming that you received the equipment in good condition.

6. Securely store the goods in the van or truck, using the rope and furniture pads, as needed.

7. Proceed with Steps 4 through 6 until all items are retrieved.

8. If the items aren't to be delivered to the shoot location at this time, make sure that they are stored securely until the time of delivery (e.g., not leaving film sitting in sunlight or exposing sensitive equipment to extreme temperatures). If storage is not needed, proceed directly to Step 9.

9. Deliver the items to the production site, making sure that each item is placed exactly where it is needed. Generally, you should unload the camera gear first, then the other items that must be used right away, then items that aren't needed until later. If you plan your pick-up route unloading will be a cinch.

10. Once the camera gear is under the watchful eye of the First Assistant Camera Operator, it's time to prepare to feed the crew.

NOTE: Promptness pays. Be on time when you are picking up or delivering items. Learning to do all aspects of your job (even the tedious ones) with a positive attitude will advance your career and make you far more marketable for future work. To truly excel as a PA, you should be pleasant and efficient and so unobtrusive that things seem magically to appear on time and in place —— out of nowhere.

CHAPTER

13

Feeding The Crew

In addition to delivering the production equipment and supplies, you are responsible for another crucial supply for the crew: food and beverages. You must ensure that the crew eats well and enjoyably. Never undervalue this crucial service to the crew. Having adequate beverages and foods available can calm irritated tempers, smooth rough edges, and make everyone on the crew more productive.

The term used for this food and beverage service is *craft service*. Several items are essential to good craft service:

1. One or two tables (or more, depending on the size of the crew and of the tables).

2. At least two coolers: one for soft drinks and one for water. Also check to see if you have access to running water. Water is a *must* if you manage never to run out of water, you'll have many allies on the set. If you don't have running water, always fill both coolers with ice first thing in the morning. Through the day, double check and refill your water supply if need be.

3. A coffee urn (full of fresh, hot coffee) and a complete supply of cups, cream, sugar, artificial sweetener, and stirrers.

4. A hot-water urn and an assortment of alternatives to coffee (e.g., tea and other beverages for those who don't drink coffee). Double check not to fill a coffee urn with hot water. Always keep the hot water urn separate. Tea and soup drinkers don't like their beverage to taste like coffee.

5. An appropriate selection of foodstuff, depending on the budget, the number of the crew members and so on.

6. Keep the area clean. Put out plenty of garbage bags. The crew should not have to search for a place to throw trash.

On shoot days, the production company hires a caterer, whom you help in setting up for the crew's breakfast. After 3-4 hours, put away the breakfast food, and bring out some snacks for munching (cheese, crakers and fruit) until it's time for lunch. After lunch the crew usually has a sweet tooth, candy and cookies. As dinner draws near try chips, dips and specialty items— anything you have left in your food hoard.

TIPS:

1. *Never* run out of water.

2. Avoid running out of food or beverages —— restock the soda coolers and replenish food trays frequently.

3. Frequently clean up around the food area, tossing out gargage, wiping spills, and otherwise making the food area appealing.

4. *Never* begin eating before the other crew members have had the chance to eat. This pratice you must accept until you have advanced and are no longer a PA.

5. Try to find out in advance how many members of the crew will be present each day, and estimate your food purchases accordingly.

Unlike the production equipment and supplies, the purchases of foodstuff will be made from petty cash, which is discussed fully in the next Chapter.

Examples of craft service foods:

Cheese	Ice
Crackers	Licorice
Gum	Sodas (diet & reg.)
Potato Chips	Paper Plates
Fruit	Plastics Untensils
Vegetables	Paper Cups
Cookies	Trash Bags
Beef Jerky	Paper Towels
Bag Candy	Toilet Paper
Water	Popcorn

(Get special requests from the Coordinator.)

CHAPTER

14

Petty Cash

As mentioned in Chapter 13, not all expenses are paid via POs (purchase orders). Foodstuffs (other than those supplied by caterers) and some props, wardrobe, hardware, rentals, fees, and other items are paid for out of "petty cash". *Petty cash* is money given to a PA by a Coordinator; the PA uses it to cover expenses incurred for completion of the job. It is money that has been budgeted for production expenses; such expenses are usually less expensive than the items purchased with a PO.

At the start of production, the Coordinator will sign out a specific amount of money for you to monitor and use as petty cash for production expenses. To underscore your responsibility for this money, the Coordinator will ask you to count the money and sign a receipt confirming the amount given to you . The amount on the receipt (called a "chit") is the amount for which you will be responsible until the end of production. At the end of production, you must return to the Coordinator exactly the same amount, either in cash receipts for purchases or in cash left over after all purchases were made. If you do not have a cash receipt for an item, you will be expected to make up the difference "out of pocket". The need for a receipt for each purchase is obvious.

Three things make it easier to track the petty cash (PC):

1. When you first receive the petty cash, put the money into a *petty cash* envelope. Be sure to note the name of the job and the job number along with your name and phone number on the envelope. Usually PC envelopes are supplied by the production company. Use that envelope for all your receipts, as well as for the cash.

2. As you acquire receipts number them in chronological order. Try to keep your numbering in the same location on the receipts, etc. lower right or upper right seem to be favored. After each receipt is numbered it will be recorded next to the corresponding number on the "Summary of job Advance Disbursements" which is the PC envelope.

3. On the PC envelope, neatly and carefully record each expenditure, noting the date, amount, category of expense, and brief explanation of the expense. It is best to use a pencil, especially if you are prone to simple numerical errors. A sample of the form is included at the end of this chapter.

NOTE: On the form, you'll notice a place to indicate "Balance Due Employee." On occasion, you may have to purchase items out of your own pocket and seek reimbursement from the production company. Avoid this if at all possible because it is not only a problem for you but also a problem for whoever figured the budget based on a smaller amount of expenses from petty cash.

Any time that you are responsible for petty cash, guard it carefully, and document each expenditure. You will go broke quickly if you have to make frequent cash compensations for items you purchased without getting receipts. Before you turn in your completed envelope and disbursements, make a copy of the expenditures for your records.

AMOUNT $_____   NO._____

RECEIVED OF PETTY CASH

_____ 19_____

FOR_____

CHARGE TO_____

APPROVED BY   RECEIVED BY

Petty cash (PC) chit.

AMOUNT $ _____   NO. _____

RECEIVED OF PETTY CASH

_____ 19 _____

FOR _____

CHARGE TO_____

_____

APPROVED BY   RECEIVED BY

_____   _____

AMOUNT $_____

RECEIVED OF PETTY CASH   NO._____

_____19_____

FOR_____

CHARGE TO _____

_____

_____   _____
APPROVED BY   RECEIVED BY

PETTY CASH

Use Separate Envelope for
Each Job Number

JOB NAME_____ JOB#_____ PAGE NO. _____

EMPLOYEE_____

EXPLANATION	DATE	AMOUNT	PROPS	TOLLS	MEALS	CAR	LUNCH	DINNER
1								
2								
3								
4								
5								
6								
7								
8								
9								
10								
11								
12								
13								
14								
15								

TOTAL DISBURSED	
AMOUNT RECEIVED	
BAL. DUE EMPLOYEE	
BAL. DUE CO.	

SIGNATURE OF EMPLOYEE _____

63

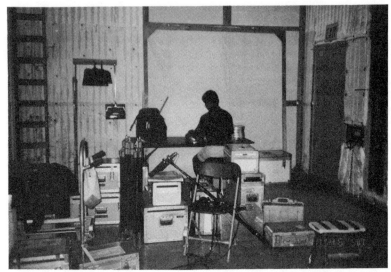

The Assistant Cameraman, down loading film, on an Emporium Capwell commercial produced by Levinson, Israelson & Bell Production Company.

Set of a Christmas commercial.

CHAPTER

15

It's a Wrap

Recall from Chapter 6 that a wrap signifies that on-site production of the movie, film, or television program is complete. It does not, however, mean that your job has ended. Chapter 12 mentioned all the duties needed for preparing for the shoot. Once shooting has ended, all those tasks must be done in reverse:

1. Get (or make) a list of all the items that must be returned (check the POs, as needed).

2. At the production site, gather up all the items to be returned, check their condition (reporting to the Coordinator any potential problems), and make sure that all the items are stored securely in the van or truck, using the rope and furniture pads (as needed) until the time of return.

65

3. Plan your route of returning the gear (modify your original route, as needed).

4. Go to each vendor, showing the equipment, and waiting for the vendor to confirm the condition of the returned items.

5. Return the van or truck to the production company, and clean it out thoroughly, returning ropes and furniture pads or other materials.

6. Once the van or truck has been cleaned, deliver it to the rental agency.

NOTE: Any time you are dealing with rented property of any kind, make sure that it is in at least as good a condition as it was when you rented it. If you don't, you could end up paying for the difference (in a cleaning bill or a repair bill). If the production company should have to pay for your indiscretion, the company may not be as eager to hire you for the next job.

Location Film Crew and Equipment Trucks.

PART FIVE

STAGE VS LOCATION

CHAPTER

16

Stage Shooting

The general guidelines for obtaining production equipment and supplies were discussed in Chapter 12. This Chapter describes how your duties change when doing *stage shooting* ——the use of a sound stage for shooting the film or video. When shooting a commercial, the production company generally rents a stage for a number of days. If the shooting is to take place on stage, the sets to be used are built on the stage, the striking of the sets will take place on stage, and the wrap will be completed on the stage. Movies and television shows may rent or the studio may assign a stage for production; the sets may be struck, saved to be reused or permanment for that production.

The stage provides the location where the production will be shot, which means that all the production supplies and equipment go straight to the stage. As you can probably guess, this arrangement makes your duties much easier than shooting on location.

The routines for stage shooting are the same as those for location shooting: deliveries, craft service, handling petty cash, and returning everything after the wrap. (Remember that being early, at least 15 minutes early is expected). When prepping for a stage shoot, try to meet with the coordinator the night before the shoot. At the meeting, discuss exactly what needs to happen in the morning at the production site.

Once you arrive at the stage and you have (a) delivered the camera gear, (b) set up the craft service (with the caterer), and (c) delivered all the other production equipment, you are ready to begin helping everyone with every conceivable task —— all at once! You can do it: Hustle, hustle, hustle. Much of the time, you may not even stay at the production site. You may have to continue running all over the countryside dropping off and picking up equipment and supplies. Learn to take your frantic work style in stride. You'll live longer and enjoy life more.

CHAPTER

17

Location Shooting

Preparing for the Shoot:

1. The day before shooting, you and the other Production Assistants and the Coordinator go over what needs to happen on location, including where things should be located.
2. The night before the shoot, you are responsible for charging (with batteries) the walkie-talkies, including an extra one to keep as a back-up in case something happens to one of them.
3. You will pick up all of the equipment (including the newly charged walkie-talkies) and load it onto the production truck (which is going to the location).
4. Your production vehicle along with one or two other vehicles may form a caravan to drive to the location.

At the Shoot:

1. Once you arrive at the location (30-45 minutes before the rest of the crew), you will mark off the parking area for the production vehicles with brightly colored parking cones.

2. You and the other PAs will set up a large sign with the production company's name and/or the name of the commercial show or film. The rest of the crew and the *talent* (the actors) will find the location based on your marking the parking area with the sign.

3. As the rest of the crew arrives, a Second AD (Assistant Director) or the lead PA will instruct everyone where to park. (Often, a police officer or fire fighter will be there to supervise).

4. You (and the other PAs) unload the camera gear, set up the craft service, help to unload everything as quickly and efficiently (but carefully) as possible. The walkie-talkies will come in handy when covering a large area. Start communicating, and start hustling right away.

NOTE: Though things are more spread out here than at the stage, the duties are basically the same as those spelled out in Chapter 12. Don't get caught standing around idly wondering what to do next. Go! Go! Go!

PART SIX

MONEY MATTERS

CHAPTER

18

Getting Paid for Your Services

Two Methods of Payment

There are two methods of getting paid by the production company: via time cards or via invoices. The actual forms used signify a lot more that just a different piece of paper. *Time cards* are submitted by an employee to an employer——that is, the production company has hired you as a full-time or part-time, temporary or permanent employee. *Invoices* are submitted by an independent contractor to a production company that has contracted to purchase specified services, often only for a specified length of time, or for a specific job.

Employees

When you are an employee, an entire body of regulations cover the ways in which your employer must treat you. One aspect of this is that the employer is required to deduct federal and state income taxes from your check before paying you. To determine the amount to deduct from your check, you are required to fill out an I.R.S. (Internal Revenue Service) W-4 form and an I-9 form. Also deducted from your check will be social security tax ("F.I.C.A."), but as an employee, the employer must contribute an equivalent amount to social security on your behalf.

If you are an employee, you must fill out a time card. On the time card, you must fill in your name, the job number, and the name of the production company for which you worked. If you are paid an hourly rate, you must carefully track the hours you work in order to record them accurately on the time card. If there is a space in which to record your hourly rate, fill that in. If, instead of an hourly rate, you are paid a flat rate, write "flat" on the time card, and record the amount of the flat rate. In either case, be sure to sign your time card at the end of the production or at the end of the week, whichever comes first, the production coordinator or accounting personnel will take your time card. Most production companies pay employees on a weekly basis.

Independent Contractors

The main advantage, for the production company, is that there are fewer goverment regulations, tax paperwork, etc.when they pay an independent contractor as verses an employee. Several other differences regarding status as an employee verses an independent contractor do not usually apply well to the PA job. For example, though independent contractors technically cannot be required to be at a specific work site during specific hours, the practical application of this may be impossible in this situation.

The major difference that applies to all independent contractors is the handling of taxes. As an independent contractor, you do not have taxes deducted from your check, and you are expected to pay estimated taxes each quarter of the year (April 15, July 15, September 15, and January 15). (If you neglect to pay estimated taxes, and owe income tax in excess of the prescribed amount, be assured that you will not only have to pay later, but you will also be assesed intrest and penalties for late payment). Also, you must pay both the employer's and the employee's share of social security tax, doubling your social security tax obligation. The Production Company doesn't pay social security tax for you, and they don't deduct your taxes from their payment to you, they still must report the money they give you to the I.R.S. For that reason, they require you to supply them with the correct information they need in order to report it accurately to the I.R.S. The following form illustrates what you might use. A simple form such as this provides all of the necessary information required by the production company when they report your payments to the I.R.S. Depending on the production company's requirements, you may be asked to file a federal form W-9 instead of or in addition to a self-contractor form.

As an independent contractor you must save all your receipts, proof of payments and keep track of your own expenses. You will need these documents to prepare your income taxes. For more information on being an independent contractor, get a copy of IRS publication 334, or consult the Small Business Association , a tax consultant or any relevant sources available to you.

Payments (Wage)

Payments vary in different parts of the world. Independent PA's seem to earn the most per day on the West Coast of the U.S. (L.A. Hollywood). New York and Florida come in close behind Los Angeles. Union work, as an employee, has less variance. Outside the U.S., wages are slightly lower, adjusting for currency exchange rates and costs of living.

In areas outside major production centers, there is less union control and PA's, as with all crew members, earn less.

A good rate of scale for the L.A. area is the following:
Independent (experienced 1 to 2 yrs.)- $125.00 to $150 a day.
Employee (staff-runner)- $250.00 to $325.00 a week.
New (less then 6 mos.)-$50.00 to $100.00 a day.

SELF - CONTRACTER FORM

PAYEE_____

ADDRESS_____

_____

S.S.# / FED. I.D. #_____

SERVICES RENDERED :

DATE:_____

RATE PER DAY : _____

FOR PERIOD: _____TO_____ TOTAL $_____

    I certify that this is a true and correct statement.

        DATE:_____ SIGNED:_____

                          CONTRACTOR

    I certify the services listed hereon were rendered and approve this

    invoice for payment.

    DATE:_____ SIGNED:_____

                TITLE:_____

    DISTRIBUTION: COMPANY NAME REPRESENTATIVE

    CHECK NO:_____   NAME:_____

    P.O. NO:_____   TITLE:_____

Timecard

Production Co._____

Employee Name_____

Soc.Sec. #_____

Union_____ Occupation _____

<table>
<tr><td colspan="3">Production
House Approval</td></tr>
</table>

Prep Wrap Shoot Code

Job# & Product	Date	Time in out	Meals in out	Rate	Str.	11/2	2x	21/2	Other	Meal Penalty	
	MON										
	TUE										
	WED										
	THU										
	FRI										
	SAT										
	SUN										
	TOTAL										

For Payroll Use Only:

Form **W-9** (Rev. December 1988) Department of the Treasury Internal Revenue Service	**Request for Taxpayer Identification Number and Certification**	**Give this form to the requester. Do NOT send to IRS.**

Please print or type

Name (If joint names, list first and circle the name of the person or entity whose number you enter in Part I below. See Instructions under "Name" if your name has changed.)

Address (number and street)

City, state, and ZIP code

List account number(s) here (optional)

Part I — Taxpayer Identification Number

Enter your taxpayer identification number in the appropriate box. For individuals and sole proprietors, this is your social security number. For other entities, it is your employer identification number. If you do not have a number, see *How To Obtain a TIN*, below.

Note: *If the account is in more than one name, see the chart on page 2 for guidelines on whose number to enter.*

Social security number

OR

Employer identification number

Part II — For Payees Exempt From Backup Withholding (See Instructions)

Requester's name and address (optional)

Certification.—Under penalties of perjury, I certify that:

(1) The number shown on this form is my correct taxpayer identification number (or I am waiting for a number to be issued to me), **and**

(2) I am not subject to backup withholding because: (a) I am exempt from backup withholding, or (b) I have not been notified by the Internal Revenue Service (IRS) that I am subject to backup withholding as a result of a failure to report all interest or dividends, or (c) the IRS has notified me that I am no longer subject to backup withholding (does not apply to real estate transactions, mortgage interest paid, the acquisition or abandonment of secured property, contributions to an individual retirement arrangement (IRA), and payments other than interest and dividends).

Certification Instructions.—You must cross out item (2) above if you have been notified by IRS that you are currently subject to backup withholding because of underreporting interest or dividends on your tax return. (Also see *Signing the Certification* under *Specific Instructions*, on page 2.)

Please Sign Here | Signature ▶ | Date ▶

Instructions

(Section references are to the Internal Revenue Code.)

Purpose of Form.—A person who is required to file an information return with IRS must obtain your correct taxpayer identification number (TIN) to report income paid to you, real estate transactions, mortgage interest paid, the acquisition or abandonment of secured property, or contributions you made to an individual retirement arrangement (IRA). Use Form W-9 to furnish your correct TIN to the requester (the person asking you to furnish your TIN), and, when applicable, (1) to certify that the TIN you are furnishing is correct (or that you are waiting for a number to be issued), (2) to certify that you are not subject to backup withholding, and (3) to claim exemption from backup withholding if you are an exempt payee. Furnishing your correct TIN and making the appropriate certifications will prevent certain payments from being subject to the 20% backup withholding.

Note: *If a requester gives you a form other than a W-9 to request your TIN, you must use the requester's form.*

How To Obtain a TIN.—If you do not have a TIN, apply for one immediately. To apply, get Form SS-5, Application for a Social Security Number Card (for individuals) from your local office of the Social Security Administration, or Form SS-4, Application for Employer Identification Number (for businesses and all other entities), from your local Internal Revenue Service office.

To complete Form W-9 if you do not have a TIN, write "Applied For" in the space for the TIN in Part I, sign and date the form, and give it to the requester. Generally, you will then have 60 days to obtain a TIN and furnish it to the requester. If the requester does not receive your TIN within 60 days, backup withholding, if applicable, will begin

and continue until you furnish your TIN to the requester. For reportable interest or dividend payments, the payer must exercise one of the following options concerning backup withholding during this 60-day period. Under option (1), a payer must backup withhold on any withdrawals you make from your account after 7 business days after the requester receives this form back from you. Under option (2), the payer must backup withhold on any reportable interest or dividend payments made to your account, regardless of whether you make any withdrawals. The backup withholding under option (2) must begin no later than 7 business days after the requester receives this form back. Under option (2) the payer is required to refund the amounts withheld if your certified TIN is received within the 60-day period and you were not subject to backup withholding during that period.

Note: *Writing "Applied For" on the form means that you have already applied for a TIN OR that you intend to apply for one in the near future.*

As soon as you receive your TIN, complete another Form W-9, include your TIN, sign and date the form, and give it to the requester.

What Is Backup Withholding?—Persons making certain payments to you are required to withhold and pay to IRS 20% of such payments under certain conditions. This is called "backup withholding." Payments that could be subject to backup withholding include interest, dividends, broker and barter exchange transactions, rents, royalties, nonemployee compensation, and certain payments from fishing boat operators, but do not include real estate transactions.

If you give the requester your correct TIN, make the appropriate certifications, and report all your taxable interest and dividends on your tax return, your payments will not be subject to backup withholding. Payments you receive will be subject to backup withholding if:

(1) You do not furnish your TIN to the requester, or

(2) IRS notifies the requester that you furnished an incorrect TIN, or

(3) You are notified by IRS that you are subject to backup withholding because you failed to report all your interest and dividends on your tax return (for interest and dividend accounts only), or

(4) You fail to certify to the requester that you are not subject to backup withholding under (3) above (for interest and dividend accounts opened after 1983 only), or

(5) You fail to certify your TIN. This applies only to interest, dividend, broker, or barter exchange accounts opened after 1983, or broker accounts considered inactive in 1983.

For other payments, you are subject to backup withholding only if (1) or (2) above applies.

Certain payees and payments are exempt from backup withholding and information reporting. See *Payees and Payments Exempt From Backup Withholding*, below, and *Exempt Payees and Payments* under *Specific Instructions*, on page 2, if you are an exempt payee.

Payees and Payments Exempt From Backup Withholding.—The following is a list of payees exempt from backup withholding and for which no information reporting is required. For interest and dividends, all listed payees are exempt except item (9). For broker transactions, payees listed in (1) through (13), and a person registered under the Investment Advisers Act of 1940 who regularly acts as a broker are exempt. Payments subject to reporting under sections 6041 and 6041A are generally exempt from backup withholding only if made to payees described in items (1) through (7), except that a corporation that provides medical and health care services or bills and collects payments for such services is not exempt from backup withholding or

Form **W-9** (Rev 12-88)

information reporting. Only payees described in items (2) through (6) are exempt from backup withholding for barter exchange transactions, patronage dividends, and payments by certain fishing boat operators.

(1) A corporation.

(2) An organization exempt from tax under section 501(a), or an individual retirement plan (IRA), or a custodial account under 403(b)(7).

(3) The United States or any of its agencies or instrumentalities.

(4) A state, the District of Columbia, a possession of the United States, or any of their political subdivisions or instrumentalities.

(5) A foreign government or any of its political subdivisions, agencies or instrumentalities.

(6) An international organization or any of its agencies or instrumentalities.

(7) A foreign central bank of issue.

(8) A dealer in securities or commodities required to register in the U.S. or a possession of the U.S.

(9) A futures commission merchant registered with the Commodity Futures Trading Commission.

(10) A real estate investment trust.

(11) An entity registered at all times during the tax year under the Investment Company Act of 1940.

(12) A common trust fund operated by a bank under section 584(a).

(13) A financial institution.

(14) A middleman known in the investment community as a nominee or listed in the most recent publication of the American Society of Corporate Secretaries, Inc., Nominee List.

(15) A trust exempt from tax under section 664 or described in section 4947.

Payments of dividends and patronage dividends generally not subject to backup withholding also include the following.

● Payments to nonresident aliens subject to withholding under section 1441.

● Payments to partnerships not engaged in a trade or business in the U.S. and that have at least one nonresident partner.

● Payments of patronage dividends not paid in money.

● Payments made by certain foreign organizations.

Payments of interest generally not subject to backup withholding include the following.

● Payments of interest on obligations issued by individuals. Note: You may be subject to backup withholding if this interest is $600 or more and is paid in the course of the payer's trade or business and you have not provided your correct TIN to the payer.

● Payments of tax-exempt interest (including exempt-interest dividends under section 852).

● Payments described in section 6049(b)(5) to nonresident aliens.

● Payments on tax-free covenant bonds under section 1451.

● Payments made by certain foreign organizations.

● Mortgage interest paid by you.

Payments that are not subject to information reporting are also not subject to backup withholding. For details, see sections 6041, 6041A(a), 6042, 6044, 6045, 6049, 6050A, and 6050N, and the regulations under such sections.

Penalties

Failure To Furnish TIN.—If you fail to furnish your correct TIN to a requester, you are subject to a penalty of $50 for each such failure unless your failure is due to reasonable cause and not to willful neglect.

Failure To Include Certain Items on Your Tax Return.—If you fail to properly include on your tax return certain items reported to IRS, such failure will be treated as being due to negligence, and you will be subject to a penalty of 5% on any part of an underpayment of tax attributable to that failure unless there is clear and convincing evidence to the contrary.

Civil Penalty for False Information With Respect to Withholding.—If you make a false statement with no reasonable basis that results in no imposition of backup withholding, you are subject to a penalty of $500.

Criminal Penalty for Falsifying Information.—Willfully falsifying certifications or affirmations may subject you to criminal penalties including fines and/or imprisonment.

Specific Instructions

Name.—If you are an individual, generally provide the name shown on your social security card. However, if you have changed your last name, for instance, due to marriage, without informing the Social Security Administration of the name change, please enter your first name and both the last name shown on your social security card and your new last name.

Signing the Certification.—

(1) **Interest, Dividend, and Barter Exchange Accounts Opened Before 1984 and Broker Accounts That Were Considered Active During 1983.**—You are not required to sign the certification; however, you may do so. You are required to provide your correct TIN.

(2) **Interest, Dividend, Broker and Barter Exchange Accounts Opened After 1983 and Broker Accounts That Were Considered Inactive During 1983.**—You must sign the certification or backup withholding will apply. If you are subject to backup withholding and you are merely providing your correct TIN to the requester, you must cross out item (2) in the certification before signing the form.

(3) **Real Estate Transactions.**—You must sign the certification. You may cross out item (2) of the certification if you wish.

(4) **Other Payments.**—You are required to furnish your correct TIN, but you are not required to sign the certification unless you have been notified of an incorrect TIN. Other payments include payments made in the course of the requester's trade or business for rents, royalties, goods (other than bills for merchandise), medical and health care services, payments to a nonemployee for services (including attorney and accounting fees), and payments to certain fishing boat crew members.

(5) **Mortgage Interest Paid by You, Acquisition or Abandonment of Secured Property, or IRA Contributions.**—You are required to furnish your correct TIN, but you are not required to sign the certification.

(6) **Exempt Payees and Payments.**—If you are exempt from backup withholding, you should complete this form to avoid possible erroneous backup withholding. Enter your correct TIN in Part I, write "EXEMPT" in the block in Part II, sign and date the form. If you are a nonresident alien or foreign entity not subject to backup withholding, give the requester a completed Form W-8, Certificate of Foreign Status.

(7) **TIN "Applied For."**—Follow the instructions under How To Obtain a TIN, on page 1, sign and date this form.

Signature.—For a joint account, only the person whose TIN is shown in Part I should sign the form.

Privacy Act Notice.—Section 6109 requires you to furnish your correct taxpayer identification number (TIN) to persons who must file information returns with IRS to report interest, dividends, and certain other income paid to you, mortgage interest you paid, the acquisition or abandonment of secured property, or contributions you made to an individual retirement arrangement (IRA). IRS uses the numbers for identification purposes and to help verify the accuracy of your tax return. You must provide your TIN whether or not you are required to file a tax return. Payers must generally withhold 20% of taxable interest, dividend, and certain other payments to a payee who does not furnish a TIN to a payer. Certain penalties may also apply.

What Name and Number To Give the Requester

For this type of account:	Give the name and SOCIAL SECURITY number of:
1. Individual	The individual
2. Two or more individuals (joint account)	The actual owner of the account or, if combined funds, the first individual on the account[1]
3. Custodian account of a minor (Uniform Gift to Minors Act)	The minor[2]
4. a. The usual revocable savings trust (grantor is also trustee)	The grantor-trustee[1]
b. So-called trust account that is not a legal or valid trust under state law	The actual owner[1]
5. Sole proprietorship	The owner[3]

For this type of account:	Give the name and EMPLOYER IDENTIFICATION number of:
6. A valid trust, estate, or pension trust	Legal entity (Do not furnish the identification number of the personal representative or trustee unless the legal entity itself is not designated in the account title.)[4]
7. Corporate	The corporation
8. Association, club, religious, charitable, educational, or other tax-exempt organization	The organization
9. Partnership	The partnership
10. A broker or registered nominee	The broker or nominee
11. Account with the Department of Agriculture in the name of a public entity (such as a state or local government, school district, or prison) that receives agricultural program payments	The public entity

[1] List first and circle the name of the person whose number you furnish.

[2] Circle the minor's name and furnish the minor's social security number.

[3] Show the name of the owner.

[4] List first and circle the name of the legal trust, estate, or pension trust.

Note: If no name is circled when there is more than one name, the number will be considered to be that of the first name listed.

★ U.S. G.P.O. 1988—205-349

82

CHAPTER

19

Mileage / Vehicle Rental

As a PA, you are often required to use your own vehicle for many of the pick-ups and deliveries. You deserve to be reimbursed for the wear and tear on your vehicle. The best way to handle this is to go to the trouble of keeping a detailed *mileage log*. You can purchase a log or use something like the following:

DATE	START MILES	END MILES	MILES TRAVELED	DESTINATION (NOTES)
8/22	35	55	20	CAMERA RENTAL HOUSE
	------	100	65	K.L EQUIPMENT
	------	120	85	JJ ' s DONUTS
8/23	150	160	10	Location

Not all companies require you to record all of your mileage, and some companies have their own mileage logs, but under no circumstances should you try to cheat a production company on the mileage you report. They have been in the business long enough to recognize when a mileage report is overly high, and a few extra dollars for mileage is not worth being fired (or never rehired) by a company.

Some companies prefer to rent your vehicle at a flat rate for the day or for the week. If so, they expect you to pay for the gas and other mileage-related expenses. If given a choice, however, you'll make out better with mileage reimbursement: it's worth the extra effort to record it accurately.

APPENDIX 1

Co-workers

This list, with brief descriptions should help you identify the job titles on a working set. (All of these titles may not be on every set.)

Executive Producer - (Executive in charge of production.) The senior financial or business production executive. (Many times the title is granted for a major financial contribution.)

Producer - The individual responsible for the creative shaping and final result of a film, television production or commercial.

Line Producer - A Producer who may work under a executive Producer, supervises most facets of production as well as the work of the production manager.

Associate Producer - An assistant to the Producer. Can be a production associate with responsibility for a specific area of production or an elevated title for a production department head eg. Associate Producer in charge of Casting. (There can be several Associate Producers on any one production.)

Director - The individual responible for realizing the intentions of the producer and the script; specifically in control of on set action and dialogue in front of the camera.

Assistant Director (AD) - The person who carries out a number or procedural duties for the director, which include scheduling shooting, calling personnel, maintaining order on the set, checking budgets, rehersing performers, coordinating with the front office and doing whatever tasks the Director may find necessary.

Second Assistant Director - The person who marks the slate and claps the sticks on the clapboard before each shot. This person is also responsible for loading the magazines.

Director Of Photography (DP) - This person is in charge of the technical requirements for lighting and photographing the production. The creative DP will also consult and assist the Director in scenic composition, technical mood, choice of camera angles, and camera set-ups.

Cameraman - The person who operates under the Director of Photography and is directly responsible for managing the camera during shooting.

Assistant Camera (AC) - The person in the camera crew who is responsible for proper maintenance of the camera during shooting. As well as checking that the camera works properly, this person is responsible for changing lenses and magazines and following focus during shooting.

Production Manager / Coordinator - The individual in charge of the daily business arrangements for shooting. He or she starts out by calculating an economical way to employ equipment, performers, locations and properties. The Production Coordinator arranges for transportation, accommodations, and meals and hires extra personnel as needed.

Art Director - The person responsible for the design and overall physical appearance of the world in which the actors appear. He may design and oversee the construction of the settings.

Costume Designer - The person who designs and coordinates the clothing worn by the characters in the production. The Costume Designer works in coordination with the Director, Art Director and sometimes with the Director of Photography.

Set Designer - The person who designs and draws the plans and writes the various specifications for each set or setting.

Set Decorator - The individual who decorates or dresses the set with props, furnishings.

Wardrobe - The person responsible for getting clothing, costumes, and accessories for the production before the actual shooting begins and for maintaining them during the actual filming.

Property Master - The individual responsible for obtaining, altering, or building properties and making sure they are available when the filming is to begin.

Gaffer - The head electrician in a film production, who is responsible for ordering, placing, operating and maintaining the required lights as well as the power source. The Gaffer has a number of electrician working under him or her.

Best Boy - The assistant to the Gaffer.

Key Grip - The head of this department. Responsible for an assortment of jobs. A Grip does an assortment of hard jobs and must have a "grip" while carrying or pushing the dolly.

Grip - The assistant to the Key Grip.

Sound Mixer - The person in charge of recording sound during the actual shooting of the production.

Boom Operator - The sound technician who operates the boom and the microphone attached to it.

Script Supervisor - The individual responsible for maintaining perfect continuity from shot to shot by keeping a record that specifies individual takes and their details.

Teleprompter Operator - The person responsible for the cuing device placed near the camera with a rotating scroll so the performers can read their lines.

Casting Director - The individual who chooses and negotiates contracts for the performers.

Make-Up - The person responsible for applying makeup to the performers in the production.

Home Economist - The person responsible for preparing the food for the on camera shooting.

Stylist - The person who takes care of the hair of both the female and males performers.

Special EFX - The person in charge for the effects achieved through special photographic techniques or processes and those specifically created before the camera when it is shooting.

VTR Operator - The person responsible for recording the image and sound on tape for playback on a television system.

Location Scout - An individual who goes in search of suitable places, either indoors or outdoors, for a production that is shooting on location.

Location Manager - An individual who contracts for their use and arranges the details of occupancy.

Craftservice - The personnel in a production that performs tasks such as obtaining coffee and snacks for the crew and performers.

APPENDIX 2

Glossary

These are terms that will help you on the set and around the industry.

ACTION- When a Director or an Assistant Director calls "Action" it means start the activity being filmed.

APERTURE- The opening gererally controlled by the diaphragm, that regulates the amount of light to pass through the lens and reach the film.

APPLE BOX- Wooden crates used to elevate tables, stands, performers etc.

ARRIFLEX- A brandname of 35mm amd 16mm cameras made by a German company.

ARTIFICIAL LIGHT- The light created for a scene, that comes from an electrical source.

BACKDROP - A large painted scene on cloth or on a flat, often seen through a door or window.

BACKGROUND ACTION - Subsidiary action taking place at the same time as the major action.

BACKING - A backdrop

BACK LOT - The area of studio ground where outdoor sets are built for exterior shooting.

BARN DOORS - A unit made up of two or four hinged doors that is attached to the front of a lamp to direct the light source.

BEAN BOARD - 4'x8' sheets of foam approx. 1" thick.

BLACKS - Any fabrics used to block out light from windows and doors, during the day to give the appearance of night.

BLOCKING - Planning the positions and movement of the performers in a scene.

BOLEX CAMERA - A lightweight hand held 16mm camera made in Switzerland.

BOOM - A long, mobile, telescopic arm with a microphone attached at one end that is held over the speaker's voice.

BOUNCE LIGHT - Lamps aimed at walls and ceiling to create diffuse light.

B-PICTURE - A cheaper made, less ambitious and less publicized film.

BUDGET - The total amount of money to be spent on a production, calculated in advance by the company.

CABLE PULLER - The individual who handles any cables attached to the camera.

CALL TIME - The time you should be on the set. Remember! If your on time your 15 minutes late.

CAMERA - The basic tool of all cinematography for photographing a series of progressive images on a strip of film.

CAMERA ANGLE - The placement of the camera in relation to the subject of the image.

CAMERA CAR - A car or truck specially designed and fitted to carry one or more cameras as well as people.

CAMERA RIGHT / CAMERA LEFT - These directions are from the camera's point of view. When facing the camera your right is the camera's left.

CAMERA SPEED - The rate per second of frames exposed in the camera.

CAMERA TAPE - Tape similar to duct or gaffer's tape comes in 1" wide rolls, mostly used by Camera Assistant to reseal cans after they were opened.

CAMERA WEDGE - A device placed upon the tripod to support the camera and allow for greater angles of tilt.

CAN - A metal or plastic circular container for storing film.

CATWALK - A narrow, railed walk suspended above the stage in the studio.

CHANGING BAG - A lightproof bag with two linings, two zippers, and sleeves on each end through which hands may extened to load film into, or unload film from the magazine.

CHINA PENCIL - A grease pencil used in editing for marking up the work print with instructions and many other uses.

CHICKEN COOP - A luminaire with six one-thousaand watt bulbs which is covered in the front by wire mesh, used as an overhead light.

CLAPBOARD - A slate with a pair of boards hinged together that is photographed at the beginning of each take. On the slate are written name of the project, Director, date, and scene number.

CLEAR THE FRAME - An order to vacate the set in front of the camera during rehearsal.

CONTINUITY - Is the proper matching of details, movement and dialogue from shot to shot .

CORE - A plastic hub of two or three inches in diameter on which film is stored.

CUE - The signal given to an actor to begin a speech or action.

CUTTING ROOM - The room where the film is edited.

CUT - Stop all the action.

C STAND - A metal stand the grip uses to hold flags.

C 47 - It's a nickname for a clothes pin.

DAILIES - The first positive prints, usually synchronized with sound, which generally are delivered by the laboratory the day after shooting.

DITTY BAG - A small canvas or leather bag that contains tools, tape, wire, etc. that a person might need on a job.

DOLLY - A mobile platform on wheels that supports the camera, allows the camera to move.

DOORWAY DOLLY - A dolly narrow enough to pass through standard doorways.

DOUBLE - A person filmed in place of a lead actor when a stunt is too dangerous or to relieve the actor from tedious technical set-ups.

DROP - A large, heavy curtain that is suspended from the fly at the rear of the set.

DUVATYNE - Is a tough canvas like black cloth. Usually used to blacken out windows.

EMULSION - The layer of light-sensitive silver salts, suspended in gelatin, which is coated on the base of film.

EXPOSED - The state of film when it has already been used in the camera.

EXTRA - An actor hired to appear in a crowd scene. They are hired day to day and receive no credit for their performance.

FADE - A gradual means of closing or starting a scene, indicates a break in action or time, or place.

FEET PER MINUTE (FPM) - The speed with which film passes through a camera.

FIRE UP - To start any equipment.

FIRST UNIT - The primary crew for a film production as opposed to the second unit.

FLAGS - Square metal frames with a rod on the end and covered in black cloth to cut light.

FLARE - A fog or glow over the image, generally caused by some strong light directly hitting the lens of the camera.

FLAT- A wooden frame covered with muslin, wood, etc. and used for scenery or as a back drop.

FLOATING WALL - A part of a wall in a set that can be removed to allow for movement of the camera.

FOG MACHINE - A portable device that can be carried by hand or placed on the ground to make controlled amounts of fog or smoke.

FOOTAGE - The measurement of film in feet.

FOREGROUND - The front area of a scene closest to the audience, where the major action takes place.

FRAMES PER SECOND - The number of frames that pass before the aperture of a camera per second.

FRAMING - The act of fitting a subject into the frame for photographing.

FREE LANCE - Any person who is independent and is not contracted to a specific production company.

FROM THE TOP - The Director's comand to start a scene from the beginning.

FX - Abbreviation for effects used to represent such terms as sound or special effects.

GATE - The part of a camera supporting the pressure plate that holds the film, on track behind the lens.

GAFFERS TAPE - 2" wide cloth tape looks like duct tape.

GEL - A transparent cellophane material; used for changing the color of light.

GENERATOR - A motor-driven machine that creates electricty as an additional source of energy for lighting a studio or on location.

GREENSMAN - The person responsible for trees, shrubs etc. on a set.

GRIP CHAIN - A lightweight chain used by the grip to fasten down an assortment of jobs.

GRIP CLIPS - Large metal reusable clothes pins.

GRIP TRUCK - A small truck employed by grips to transport equipment or props.

HALF APPLE - A box, half the weight of an apple box.

HAND MODEL - A individual whose hands alone are photographed.

HAND PROPS - Small items such as books, pens, cups used by performers during shooting.

HEAD SHOT - A shot in which the frame is largely taken up with the head of the performer.

HIT THE JUICE -A direction to turn on the lights for shooting.

HIT THE MARK - A direction for an actor to move to a previously designated mark on the floor.

HONEYWAGON - Mobile vehicle with restrooms.

HOT SET - A set all prepared for shooting, with scenery and props in exact position and lighting for use. The set should not be entered while hot or with Red light flashing.

HOUSE LIGHTS - The general lights in a studio exclusive of those used on the set for filming.

INDEPENDENT FILM - A motion picure made by a filmmaker who has no connection with the Hollywood scene.

INDEPENDENT PRODUCER - An individual who produces independently and is not under contract to a studio or production company.

IN- HOUSE UNIT - A production unit that belongs to the company rather than one hired for a single production.

INSERT STAGE - A small studio employed for photographing close-ups of objects that will be inserted into the film.

IN SHOT - Any person or object accidentally in a shot.

IN THE CAN - The term that the shooting of the entire project is finished.

JUICER - Slang for an electrican.

KILL - To turn something off.

LAB - The place where film is developed and printed at the

various stages of the production.

LAYOUT BOARD - A thin piece of card board that comes in 4'x8' sheets, used to cover a surface to save it from being marked up.

LIVE ACTION - Events in a production performed by living people as distinguished from those performed by animated fiqures.

LOAD - To place unexposed film in a camera or camera magazines.

LOCATION - Any place other then a studio where a production is in part or completely shot.

LOT - The outdoor area of a studio where sets are constructed or stored and where filming somtimes takes place.

LOW-BUDGET PRODUCTION - The making of a production with a limited amount of money.

MAGAZINE - A light-proof container that feeds the film into the camera.

MAGIC HOUR - The brief period of dawn and dusk that allow enough light for shooting.

MOS - Initals printed on a clapboard and appearing at the start of a take to indicate that the scene was shoot without sound.

MOVIEOLA - A portable machine to screen dailies and edit film.

NAGRA - A synchronous tape recorder used in the business.

NATURAL LIGHTING - The term is most often used to describe daylight or illumination from the sun.

NG TAKE - A take which is "no good" and not usable.

NO PRINT - An instruction on a camera report to the lab that a certain take should not be printed.

OK TAKES - Takes that are satisfactory and should be delveloped.

ON CAMERA - Any object or performer visible in the camera's field during shooting.

OUT TAKE - A shot not used in the final version of the project.

PARALLELS - Portable scaffolding to elevate camera or lighting equipment.

PICK-UP SHOT - The shot taken from a point where the previous shot has ended.

PLAYBACK - The playing of images (and often sound) from a videotape that have just been recorded from the scene.

PRINT IT - The order given by the Director when he or she is satisfied with the take.

PROMO - An abbrevition and a slang for "promotion" which means a type of publicity for a project.

PROP BOX - A container with smaller props needed for a day's shooting.

RED LIGHT - The camera is rolling. Wait for red light to stop flashing before entering the stage.

RELOAD - To place another film magazine in the camera or tape in the recorder.

RETAKE - To reshoot a scene because the previous take was unsatisfactory.

ROLL CAMERA - The order from the Director or Assistant Director to start the camera.

ROLLING - The filming has started. The film is moving through the camera.

SAFETY SHOT - A second shot of a scene made for insurance in case the previous shot might be faulty.

SANDBAG - A heavy canvas bag filled with sand, used to support equipment at the base.

SCENE DOCK - The place in a studio where parts of a set used for scenery are stored.

SCRATCH - A mark or cut in the form of a thin line that appears on the emulsion or base of a film.

SECOND UNIT - A small unit of film technicians, subsidiary to the principle film unit.

SET - An artiifically constructed place for the action of the film or commercial.

SHORT END - The unexposed film that remains in the magazine of the camera after shooting because it is too short to use for another complete shot.

SHOT LIST - A list of all the shots in the order in which they were photographed during filming.

SHOW CARD - Comes in 32'x40' cards. It is used to bounce light off of.

SILK - A diffuser, made of a stretched piece of white material on a frame.

SOFT - Unsharp images, doesn't sharply define the objects.

SOUND STAGE - A special studio for shooting a film and recording sound.

SPEC - Working for free or for anticipated future payment.

SPOOL - A plastic or metal cylindrical device on which film is wound with flanges on the sides of the spool protecting the edges of the film.

SOURCE BOOK - Is your personal book of the names and phone numbers (people, producion companies, rental houses, etc.) that you have acquired over a period of time.

STOCK - Unexposed film also referred to as raw stock.

SWING GANG - Personnel from the film crew who work at night readying the set for the next day's filming.

SYNC - A term used in film that relates to synchronized sound and picture.

TAG - The final scene on a film, after the climax, that ties up all the action.

TAILS OUT - This term refers to a reel of film or tape with the end on the outside.

TAIL SLATE - The slate that marks a shot at the end of the take instead of the beginning.

THREAD UP - To position film so that it will run properly in its path through a piece of film machinery.

TRIPOD - A three-legged support for the camera made of hardwood or stainless steel.

UPSTAGE - The rear part of the stage.

VISQUEENE - Plastic that comes in different thickness, usually clear or black. Used to cover things.

WALK-AWAY - Leave the set and or stage (A "wrap" is not required) filming will resume the following day.

WEDGES - A piece of wood 10"x4"x 1/16" tapers to 1" thick.

WESTERN DOLLY - A transport for a camera during shooting that can carry a heavy load.

WILD TRACK - A sound track not recorded in synchronization with the shooting of a scene.

WORK PRINT - A print made from the original negative. This is what is picked up at the lab, the next day for screening.

WRAP - The completion of the production's shooting for that day or for the entire films completion.

WRONG SET - A term indicating that a set is no longer needed for shooting, and that it is time to start shooting on the next set.

Titles of Related Interest

WRITING FOR DOUGH
Adventures of a T.V. Comedy Writer
by Bill Idelson

HOWARD HAWKS
by Clark Branson
with foreword by Judith Harte

THE BRIDE OF FILM BOOK
REFERENCE GUIDE
by David McDaniel

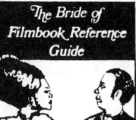

Available at bookstores or direct from:

PLAYERS PRESS
P.O. Box 1132
Studio City, CA 91614-0132